THREE SUNSETS
AND OTHER POEMS

MAVEN BOOKS

THREE SUNSETS
AND OTHER POEMS

LEWIS CARROLL

MAVEN BOOKS

Chennai   Trichy   Tirunelveli   New Delhi

MAVEN BOOKS

An imprint of **MJP Publishers**

ISBN 978-93-87867-90-1   **MAVEN Books**

All rights reserved   No. 44, Nallathambi Street,
Printed and bound in India   Triplicane, Chennai 600 005

MJP 812   © Publishers, 2020

Publisher : C. Janarthanan

PUBLISHER'S NOTE

The legacy of a country is in its varied cultural heritage, historical literature, developments in the field of economy and science. The top nations in the world are competing in the field of science, economy and literature. This vast legacy has to be conserved and documented so that it can be bestowed to the future generation. The knowledge of this legacy is slowly getting perished in the present generation due to lack of documentation.

Keeping this in mind, the concern with retrospective acquiring of rare books has been accented recently by the burgeoning reprint industry. MAVEN Books is gratified to retrieve the rare collections with a view to bring back those books that were landmarks in their time.

In this effort, a series of rare books would be republished under the banner, "MAVEN Books". The books in the reprint series have been carefully selected for their contemporary usefulness as well as their historical importance within the intellectual. We reconstruct the book with slight enhancements made for better presentation, without affecting the contents of the original edition.

Most of the works selected for republishing covers a huge range of subjects, from history to anthropology. We believe this reprint edition will be a service to the numerous researchers and practitioners active in this fascinating field. We allow readers to experience the wonder of peering into a scholarly work of the highest order and seminal significance.

MAVEN Books

PREFACE

Nearly the whole of this volume is a reprint of the serious portion of *Phantasmagoria and other Poems*, which was first published in 1869 and has long been out of print. "The Path of Roses" was written soon after the Crimean War, when the name of Florence Nightingale had already become a household-word. "Only a Woman's Hair" was suggested by a circumstance mentioned in *The Life of Dean Swift*, viz., that, after his death, a small packet was found among his papers, containing a single lock of hair and inscribed with those words. "After Three Days" was written after seeing Holman Hunt's picture, *The Finding of Christ in the Temple*.

The two poems, "Far Away" and "A Song of Love", are reprinted from *Sylvie and Bruno* and *Sylvie and Bruno Concluded*, books whose high price (made necessary by the great cost of production) has, I fear, put them out of the reach of most of my readers. "A Lesson in Latin" is reprinted from *The Jabberwock*, a Magazine got up among the Members of "The Girls' Latin School, Boston, U.S.A." The only poems, here printed for the first time, are put together under the title of "Puck Lost and Found," having been inscribed in two books—*Fairies*, a poem by Allingham, illustrated by Miss E. Gertrude Thomson, and *Merry Elves*, a story-book, by whom written I do not know, illustrated by C. O. Murray—which were presented to a little girl and boy, as a sort of memento of a visit paid by them to the author one day, on which occasion he taught them the pastime—dear to the hearts of children—of folding paper-"pistols," which can be made to imitate, fairly well, the noise of a real one.

Jan., 1898.

CONTENTS

Three Sunsets	1
The Path of Roses	5
The Valley of the Shadow of Death	9
Solitude	13
Far Away	15
Beatrice	17
Stolen Waters	19
The Willow-Tree	24
Only a Woman's Hair	25
The Sailor's Wife	27
After Three Days	30
Faces in the Fire	33
A Lesson in Latin	35
Puck Lost and Found	36
A Song of Love	38

THREE SUNSETS

He saw her once, and in the glance,
    A moment's glance of meeting eyes,
His heart stood still in sudden trance:
    He trembled with a sweet surprise—
All in the waning light she stood,
The star of perfect womanhood.

That summer-eve his heart was light:
    With lighter step he trod the ground:
And life was fairer in his sight,
    And music was in every sound:
He blessed the world where there could be
So beautiful a thing as she.

There once again, as evening fell
    And stars were peering overhead,
Two lovers met to bid farewell:
    The western sun gleamed faint and red,
Lost in a drift of purple cloud
That wrapped him like a funeral-shroud.

Long time the memory of that night—
    The hand that clasped, the lips that kissed,
The form that faded from his sight
    Slow sinking through the tearful mist—
In dreamy music seemed to roll
Through the dark chambers of his soul.

So after many years he came
    A wanderer from a distant shore:
The street, the house, were still the same,
    But those he sought were there no more:
His burning words, his hopes and fears,
Unheeded fell on alien ears.

Only the children from their play
   Would pause the mournful tale to hear,
Shrinking in half-alarm away,
   Or, step by step, would venture near
To touch with timid curious hands
That strange wild man from other lands.

He sat beside the busy street,
   There, where he last had seen her face:
And thronging memories, bitter-sweet,
   Seemed yet to haunt the ancient place:
Her footfall ever floated near:
Her voice was ever in his ear.

He sometimes, as the daylight waned
   And evening mists began to roll,
In half-soliloquy complained
   Of that black shadow on his soul,
And blindly fanned, with cruel care,
The ashes of a vain despair.

The summer fled: the lonely man
   Still lingered out the lessening days;
Still, as the night drew on, would scan
   Each passing face with closer gaze—
Till, sick at heart, he turned away,
And sighed "she will not come to-day."

So by degrees his spirit bent
   To mock its own despairing cry,
In stern self-torture to invent
   New luxuries of agony,
And people all the vacant space
With visions of her perfect face.

Then for a moment she was nigh,
   He heard no step, but she was there;
As if an angel suddenly
   Were bodied from the viewless air,
And all her fine ethereal frame
Should fade as swiftly as it came.

So, half in fancy's sunny trance,
    And half in misery's aching void
With set and stony countenance
    His bitter being he enjoyed,
And thrust for ever from his mind
The happiness he could not find.

As when the wretch, in lonely room,
    To selfish death is madly hurled,
The glamour of that fatal fume
    Shuts out the wholesome living world—
So all his manhood's strength and pride
One sickly dream had swept aside.

Yea, brother, and we passed him there,
    But yesterday, in merry mood,
And marveled at the lordly air
    That shamed his beggar's attitude,
Nor heeded that ourselves might be
Wretches as desperate as he;

Who let the thought of bliss denied
    Make havoc of our life and powers,
And pine, in solitary pride,
    For peace that never shall be ours,
Because we will not work and wait
In trustful patience for our fate.

And so it chanced once more that she
    Came by the old familiar spot:
The face he would have died to see
    Bent o'er him, and he knew it not;
Too rapt in selfish grief to hear,
Even when happiness was near.

And pity filled her gentle breast
    For him that would not stir nor speak
The dying crimson of the west,
    That faintly tinged his haggard cheek,
Fell on her as she stood, and shed
A glory round the patient head.

Ah, let him wake! The moments fly:
   This awful tryst may be the last.
And see, the tear, that dimmed her eye,
   Had fallen on him ere she passed—
She passed: the crimson paled to gray:
And hope departed with the day.

The heavy hours of night went by,
   And silence quickened into sound,
And light slid up the eastern sky,
   And life began its daily round—
But light and life for him were fled:
His name was numbered with the dead.

Nov., 1861.

THE PATH OF ROSES

In the dark silence of an ancient room,
Whose one tall window fronted to the West,
Where, through laced tendrils of a hanging vine,
The sunset-glow was fading into night,
Sat a pale Lady, resting weary hands
Upon a great clasped volume, and her face
Within her hands. Not as in rest she bowed,
But large hot tears were coursing down her cheek,
And her low-panted sobs broke awefully
Upon the sleeping echoes of the night.
    Soon she unclasp'd the volume once again,
And read the words in tone of agony,
As in self-torture, weeping as she read:—

"He crowns the glory of his race:
He prayeth but in some fit place
To meet his foeman face to face:

"And, battling for the True, the Right,
From ruddy dawn to purple night,
To perish in the midmost fight:

"Where hearts are fierce and hands are strong,
Where peals the bugle loud and long,
Where blood is dropping in the throng:

"Still, with a dim and glazing eye,
To watch the tide of victory,
To hear in death the battle-cry:

"Then, gathered grandly to his grave,
To rest among the true and brave,
In holy ground, where yew-trees wave:

"Where, from church-windows sculptured fair,
Float out upon the evening air
The note of praise, the voice of prayer:

"Where no vain marble mockery
Insults with loud and boastful lie
The simple soldier's memory:

"Where sometimes little children go,
And read, in whisper'd accent slow,
The name of him who sleeps below."

Her voice died out: like one in dreams she sat.
"Alas!" she sighed. "For what can Woman do?
Her life is aimless, and her death unknown:
Hemmed in by social forms she pines in vain.
Man has his work, but what can Woman do?"
    And answer came there from the creeping gloom,
The creeping gloom that settled into night:
"Peace! For thy lot is other than a man's:
His is a path of thorns: he beats them down:
He faces death: he wrestles with despair.
Thine is of roses, to adorn and cheer
His lonely life, and hide the thorns in flowers."
    She spake again: in bitter tone she spake:
"Aye, as a toy, the puppet of an hour,
Or a fair posy, newly plucked at morn,
But flung aside and withered ere the night."
    And answer came there from the creeping gloom,
The creeping gloom that blackened into night:
"So shalt thou be the lamp to light his path,
What time the shades of sorrow close around."
    And, so it seemed to her, an awful light
Pierced slowly through the darkness, orbed, and grew,
Until all passed away—the ancient room—
The sunlight dying through the trellised vine—
The one tall window—all had passed away,
And she was standing on the mighty hills.
    Beneath, around, and far as eye could see,
Squadron on squadron, stretched opposing hosts,
Ranked as for battle, mute and motionless.
Anon a distant thunder shook the ground,

The tramp of horses, and a troop shot by—
Plunged headlong in that living sea of men—
Plunged to their death: back from that fatal field
A scattered handful, fighting hard for life,
Broke through the serried lines; but, as she gazed,
They shrank and melted, and their forms grew thin—
Grew pale as ghosts when the first morning ray
Dawns from the East—the trumpet's brazen blare
Died into silence—and the vision passed—
Passed to a room where sick and dying lay
In long, sad line—there brooded Fear and Pain—
Darkness was there, the shade of Azrael's wing.
But there was one that ever, to and fro,
Moved with light footfall: purely calm her face,
And those deep steadfast eyes that starred the gloom:
Still, as she went, she ministered to each
Comfort and counsel; cooled the fevered brow
With softest touch, and in the listening ear
Of the pale sufferer whispered words of peace.
The dying warrior, gazing as she passed,
Clasped his thin hands and blessed her. Bless her too,
Thou, who didst bless the merciful of old!
   So prayed the Lady, watching tearfully
Her gentle moving onward, till the night
Had veiled her wholly, and the vision passed.
   Then once again the solemn whisper came:
"So in the darkest path of man's despair,
Where War and Terror shake the troubled earth,
Lies woman's mission; with unblenching brow
To pass through scenes of horror and affright
Where men grow sick and tremble: unto her
All things are sanctified, for all are good.
Nothing so mean, but shall deserve her care:
Nothing so great, but she may bear her part.
No life is vain: each hath his place assigned:
Do thou thy task, and leave the rest to God."
And there was silence, but the Lady made
No answer, save one deeply-breathed "Amen."
   And she arose, and in that darkening room
Stood lonely as a spirit of the night—
Stood calm and fearless in the gathered night—
And raised her eyes to heaven. There were tears

Upon her face, but in her heart was peace,
Peace that the world nor gives nor takes away!

April 10, 1856.

THE VALLEY OF
THE SHADOW OF DEATH

Hark, *said the dying man, and sighed,*
    To that complaining tone—
Like sprite condemned, each eventide,
    To walk the world alone.
At sunset, when the air is still,
I hear it creep from yonder hill:
It breathes upon me, dead and chill,
    A moment, and is gone.

My son, it minds me of a day
    Left half a life behind,
That I have prayed to put away
    For ever from my mind.
But bitter memory will not die:
It haunts my soul when none is nigh:
I hear its whisper in the sigh
    Of that complaining wind.

And now in death my soul is fain
    To tell the tale of fear
That hidden in my breast hath lain
    Through many a weary year:
Yet time would fail to utter all—
The evil spells that held me thrall,
And thrust my life from fall to fall,
    Thou needest not to hear.

The spells that bound me with a chain,
    Sin's stern behests to do,
Till Pleasure's self, invoked in vain,
    A heavy burden grew—
Till from my spirit's fevered eye,
A hunted thing, I seemed to fly

Through the dark woods that underlie
    Yon mountain-range of blue.

Deep in those woods I found a vale
    No sunlight visiteth,
Nor star, nor wandering moonbeam pale;
    Where never comes the breath
Of summer-breeze—there in mine ear,
Even as I lingered half in fear,
I heard a whisper, cold and clear,
    "This is the gate of Death.

"O bitter is it to abide
    In weariness alway:
At dawn to sigh for eventide,
    At eventide for day.
Thy noon hath fled: thy sun hath shone.
The brightness of thy day is gone:
What need to lag and linger on
    Till life be cold and gray?

"O well," it said, "beneath yon pool,
    In some still cavern deep,
The fevered brain might slumber cool,
    The eyes forget to weep:
Within that goblet's mystic rim
Are draughts of healing, stored for him
Whose heart is sick, whose sight is dim,
    Who prayeth but to sleep!"

The evening-breeze went moaning by,
    Like mourner for the dead,
And stirred, with shrill complaining sigh,
    The tree-tops overhead:
My guardian-angel seemed to stand
And mutely wave a warning hand—
With sudden terror all unmanned,
    I turned myself and fled!

A cottage-gate stood open wide:
    Soft fell the dying ray
On two fair children, side by side,
    That rested from their play—

Together bent the earnest head,
As ever and anon they read
From one dear Book: the words they said
      Come back to me to-day.

Like twin cascades on mountain-stair
      Together wandered down
The ripples of the golden hair,
      The ripples of the brown:
While, through the tangled silken haze,
Blue eyes looked forth in eager gaze,
More starlike than the gems that blaze
      About a monarch's crown.

My son, there comes to each an hour
      When sinks the spirit's pride—
When weary hands forget their power
      The strokes of death to guide:
In such a moment, warriors say,
A word the panic-rout may stay,
A sudden charge redeem the day
      And turn the living tide.

I could not see, for blinding tears,
      The glories of the west:
A heavenly music filled mine ears,
      A heavenly peace my breast.
"Come unto Me, come unto Me—
All ye that labour, unto Me—
Ye heavy-laden, come to Me—
      And I will give you rest."

The night drew onward: thin and blue
      The evening mists arise
To bathe the thirsty land in dew,
      As erst in Paradise—
While, over silent field and town,
The deep blue vault of heaven looked down;
Not, as of old, in angry frown,
      But bright with angels' eyes.

Blest day! Then first I heard the voice
      That since hath oft beguiled

These eyes from tears, and bid rejoice
    This heart with anguish wild—
Thy mother, boy, thou hast not known;
So soon she left me here to moan—
Left me to weep and watch, alone,
    Our one beloved child.

Though, parted from my aching sight,
    Like homeward-speeding dove,
She passed into the perfect light
    That floods the world above;
Yet our twin spirits, well I know—
Though one abide in pain below—
Love, as in summers long ago,
    And evermore shall love.

So with a glad and patient heart
    I move toward mine end:
The streams, that flow awhile apart,
    Shall both in ocean blend.
I dare not weep: I can but bless
The Love that pitied my distress,
And lent me, in Life's wilderness,
    So sweet and true a friend.

But if there be—O if there be
    A truth in what they say,
That angel-forms we cannot see
    Go with us on our way;
Then surely she is with me here,
I dimly feel her spirit near—
The morning-mists grow thin and clear,
    And Death brings in the Day.

April, 1868.

SOLITUDE

I love the stillness of the wood:
   I love the music of the rill:
I love to couch in pensive mood
      Upon some silent hill.

Scarce heard, beneath yon arching trees,
   The silver-crested ripples pass;
And, like a mimic brook, the breeze
      Whispers among the grass.

Here from the world I win release,
   Nor scorn of men, nor footstep rude,
Break in to mar the holy peace
      Of this great solitude.

Here may the silent tears I weep
   Lull the vexed spirit into rest,
As infants sob themselves to sleep
      Upon a mother's breast.

But when the bitter hour is gone,
   And the keen throbbing pangs are still,
Oh sweetest then to couch alone
      Upon some silent hill!

To live in joys that once have been,
   To put the cold world out of sight,
And deck life's drear and barren scene
      With hues of rainbow-light.

For what to man the gift of breath,
   If sorrow be his lot below;
If all the day that ends in death
      Be dark with clouds of woe?

Shall the poor transport of an hour
    Repay long years of sore distress—
The fragrance of a lonely flower
        Make glad the wilderness?

Ye golden hours of Life's young spring,
    Of innocence, of love and truth!
Bright, beyond all imagining,
        Thou fairy-dream of youth!

I'd give all wealth that years have piled,
    The slow result of Life's decay,
To be once more a little child
        For one bright summer-day.

March 16, 1853.

FAR AWAY

He stept so lightly to the land,
    All in his manly pride:
He kissed her cheek, he clasped her hand;
    Yet still she glanced aside.
"Too gay he seems," she darkly dreams,
    "Too gallant and too gay,
To think of me—poor simple me—
    When he is far away!"

"I bring my Love this goodly pearl
    Across the seas," he said:
"A gem to deck the dearest girl
    That ever sailor wed!"
She holds it tight: her eyes are bright:
    Her throbbing heart would say
"He thought of me—he thought of me—
    When he was far away!"

The ship has sailed into the West:
    Her ocean-bird is flown:
A dull dead pain is in her breast,
    And she is weak and lone:
But there's a smile upon her face,
    A smile that seems to say
"He'll think of me—he'll think of me—
    When he is far away!

"Though waters wide between us glide,
    Our lives are warm and near:
No distance parts two faithful hearts—
    Two hearts that love so dear:
And I will trust my sailor-lad,
    For ever and a day,
To think of me—to think of me—
    When he is far away!"

BEATRICE

In her eyes is the living light
   Of a wanderer to earth
From a far celestial height:
      Summers five are all the span—
      Summers five since Time began
To veil in mists of human night
   A shining angel-birth.

Does an angel look from her eyes?
   Will she suddenly spring away,
And soar to her home in the skies?
      Beatrice! Blessing and blessed to be!
      Beatrice! Still, as I gaze on thee,
Visions of two sweet maids arise,
   Whose life was of yesterday:

Of a Beatrice pale and stern,
   With the lips of a dumb despair,
With the innocent eyes that yearn—
      Yearn for the young sweet hours of life,
      Far from sorrow and far from strife,
For the happy summers, that never return,
   When the world seemed good and fair:

Of a Beatrice glorious, bright—
   Of a sainted, ethereal maid,
Whose blue eyes are deep fountains of light,
      Cheering the poet that broodeth apart,
      Filling with gladness his desolate heart,
Like the moon when she shines thro' a cloudless night
   On a world of silence and shade.

And the visions waver and faint,
   And the visions vanish away
That my fancy delighted to paint—
      She is here at my side, a living child,
      With the glowing cheek and the tresses wild,

Nor death-pale martyr, nor radiant saint,
  Yet stainless and bright as they.

For I think, if a grim wild beast
  Were to come from his charnel-cave,
From his jungle-home in the East—
    Stealthily creeping with bated breath,
    Stealthily creeping with eyes of death—
He would all forget his dream of the feast,
  And crouch at her feet a slave.

She would twine her hand in his mane:
  She would prattle in silvery tone,
Like the tinkle of summer-rain—
    Questioning him with her laughing eyes,
    Questioning him with a glad surprise,
Till she caught from those fierce eyes again
  The love that lit her own.

And be sure, if a savage heart,
  In a mask of human guise,
Were to come on her here apart—
    Bound for a dark and a deadly deed,
    Hurrying past with pitiless speed—
He would suddenly falter and guiltily start
  At the glance of her pure blue eyes.

Nay, be sure, if an angel fair,
  A bright seraph undefiled,
Were to stoop from the trackless air,
    Fain would she linger in glad amaze—
    Lovingly linger to ponder and gaze,
With a sister's love and a sister's care,
  On the happy, innocent child.

Dec. 4, 1862.

STOLEN WATERS

The light was faint, and soft the air
        That breathed around the place;
And she was lithe, and tall, and fair,
        And with a wayward grace
        Her queenly head she bare.

With glowing cheek, with gleaming eye,
        She met me on the way:
My spirit owned the witchery
        Within her smile that lay:
I followed her, I knew not why.

The trees were thick with many a fruit,
        The grass with many a flower:
My soul was dead, my tongue was mute,
        In that accursëd hour.

And, in my dream, with silvery voice,
        She said, or seemed to say,
"Youth is the season to rejoice—"
        I could not choose but stay:
        I could not say her nay.

She plucked a branch above her head,
        With rarest fruitage laden:
"Drink of the juice, Sir Knight," she said:
        "'Tis good for knight and maiden."

Oh, blind mine eye that would not trace—
   Oh, deaf mine ear that would not heed—
The mocking smile upon her face,
        The mocking voice of greed!

I drank the juice; and straightway felt
        A fire within my brain:

My soul within me seemed to melt
        In sweet delirious pain.

"Sweet is the stolen draught," she said:
        "Hath sweetness stint or measure?
Pleasant the secret hoard of bread:
        What bars us from our pleasure?"

"Yea, take we pleasure while we may,"
        I heard myself replying.
In the red sunset, far away,
        My happier life was dying:
My heart was sad, my voice was gay.

And unawares, I knew not how,
    I kissed her dainty finger-tips,
I kissed her on the lily brow,
    I kissed her on the false, false lips—
That burning kiss, I feel it now!

"True love gives true love of the best:
    Then take," I cried, "my heart to thee!"
The very heart from out my breast
    I plucked, I gave it willingly:
    Her very heart she gave to me—
Then died the glory from the west.

In the gray light I saw her face,
    And it was withered, old, and gray;
The flowers were fading in their place,
    Were fading with the fading day.

Forth from her, like a hunted deer,
    Through all that ghastly night I fled,
And still behind me seemed to hear
        Her fierce unflagging tread;
And scarce drew breath for fear.

Yet marked I well how strangely seemed
    The heart within my breast to sleep:
Silent it lay, or so I dreamed,
        With never a throb or leap.

For hers was now my heart, she said,
   The heart that once had been mine own:
And in my breast I bore instead
      A cold, cold heart of stone.
So grew the morning overhead.

The sun shot downward through the trees
     His old familiar flame:
All ancient sounds upon the breeze
      From copse and meadow came—
      But I was not the same.

They call me mad: I smile, I weep,
     Uncaring how or why:
Yea, when one's heart is laid asleep,
      What better than to die?
So that the grave be dark and deep.

To die! To die? And yet, methinks,
     I drink of life, to-day,
Deep as the thirsty traveler drinks
      Of fountain by the way:
My voice is sad, my heart is gay.

When yestereve was on the wane,
     I heard a clear voice singing
So sweetly that, like summer-rain,
      My happy tears came springing:
My human heart returned again.

    "A rosy child,
Sitting and singing, in a garden fair,
    The joy of hearing, seeing,
    The simple joy of being—
Or twining rosebuds in the golden hair
    That ripples free and wild.

    "A sweet pale child—
Wearily looking to the purple West—
    Waiting the great For-ever
    That suddenly shall sever

The cruel chains that hold her from her rest—
  By earth-joys unbeguiled.

  "An angel-child—
Gazing with living eyes on a dead face:
    The mortal form forsaken,
    That none may now awaken,
That lieth painless, moveless in her place,
    As though in death she smiled!

  "Be as a child—
So shalt thou sing for very joy of breath—
    So shalt thou wait thy dying,
    In holy transport lying—
So pass rejoicing through the gate of death,
    In garment undefiled."

Then call me what they will, I know
        That now my soul is glad:
If this be madness, better so,
        Far better to be mad,
Weeping or smiling as I go.

For if I weep, it is that now
    I see how deep a loss is mine,
And feel how brightly round my brow
        The coronal might shine,
Had I but kept mine early vow:

And if I smile, it is that now
    I see the promise of the years—
The garland waiting for my brow,
        That must be won with tears,
With pain—with death—I care not how.

May 9, 1862.

THE WILLOW-TREE

The morn was bright, the steeds were light,
    The wedding guests were gay:
Young Ellen stood within the wood
    And watched them pass away.
She scarcely saw the gallant train:
    The tear-drop dimmed her ee:
Unheard the maiden did complain
    Beneath the Willow-Tree.

"Oh Robin, thou didst love me well,
    Till, on a bitter day,
She came, the Lady Isabel,
    And stole thy heart away.
My tears are vain: I live again
    In days that used to be,
When I could meet thy welcome feet
    Beneath the Willow-Tree.

"Oh Willow gray, I may not stay
    Till Spring renew thy leaf;
But I will hide myself away,
    And nurse a lonely grief.
It shall not dim Life's joy for him:
    My tears he shall not see:
While he is by, I'll come not nigh
    My weeping Willow-Tree.

"But when I die, oh let me lie
    Beneath thy loving shade,
That he may loiter careless by,
    Where I am lowly laid.
And let the white white marble tell,
    If he should stoop to see,
'Here lies a maid that loved thee well,
    Beneath the Willow-Tree.'"

1859.

ONLY A WOMAN'S HAIR

'Only a woman's hair'! Fling it aside!
   A bubble on Life's mighty stream:
Heed it not, man, but watch the broadening tide
      Bright with the western beam.

Nay! In those words there rings from other years
   The echo of a long low cry,
Where a proud spirit wrestles with its tears
      In loneliest agony.

And, as I touch that lock, strange visions throng
   Upon my soul with dreamy grace—
Of woman's hair, the theme of poet's song
      In every time and place.

A child's bright tresses, by the breezes kissed
   To sweet disorder as she flies,
Veiling, beneath a cloud of golden mist,
      Flushed cheek and laughing eyes—

Or fringing, like a shadow, raven-black,
   The glory of a queen-like face—
Or from a gipsy's sunny brow tossed back
      In wild and wanton grace—

Or crown-like on the hoary head of Age,
   Whose tale of life is well-nigh told—
Or, last, in dreams I make my pilgrimage
      To Bethany of old.

I see the feast—the purple and the gold—
   The gathering crowd of Pharisees,
Whose scornful eyes are centred to behold
      Yon woman on her knees.

The stifled sob rings strangely on mine ears,
    Wrung from the depth of sin's despair:
And still she bathes the sacred feet with tears,
    And wipes them with her hair.

He scorned not then the simple loving deed
    Of her, the lowest and the last;
Then scorn not thou, but use with earnest heed
    This relic of the past.

The eyes that loved it once no longer wake:
    So lay it by with reverent care—
Touching it tenderly for sorrow's sake—
    It is a woman's hair.

Feb. 17, 1862.

THE SAILOR'S WIFE

See! There are tears upon her face—
　　Tears newly shed, and scarcely dried:
Close, in an agonised embrace,
　　She clasps the infant at her side.

Peace dwells in those soft-lidded eyes,
　　Those parted lips that faintly smile—
Peace, the foretaste of Paradise,
　　In heart too young for care or guile.

No peace that mother's features wear;
　　But quivering lip, and knotted brow,
And broken mutterings, all declare
　　The fearful dream that haunts her now.

The storm-wind, rushing through the sky,
　　Wails from the depths of cloudy space;
Shrill, piercing as the seaman's cry
　　When death and he are face to face.

Familiar tones are in the gale:
　　They ring upon her startled ear:
And quick and low she pants the tale
　　That tells of agony and fear:

"Still that phantom-ship is nigh—
　　With a vexed and life-like motion,
All beneath an angry sky,
　　Rocking on an angry ocean.

"Round the straining mast and shrouds
　　Throng the spirits of the storm:
Darkly seen through driving clouds,
　　Bends each gaunt and ghastly form.

"See! The good ship yields at last!
    Dumbly yields, and fights no more;
Driving, in the frantic blast,
    Headlong on the fatal shore.

"Hark! I hear her battered side,
    With a low and sullen shock,
Dashed, amid the foaming tide,
    Full upon a sunken rock.

"His face shines out against the sky,
    Like a ghost, so cold and white;
With a dead despairing eye
    Gazing through the gathered night.

"Is he watching, through the dark
    Where a mocking ghostly hand
Points a faint and feeble spark
    Glimmering from the distant land?

"Sees he, in this hour of dread,
    Hearth and home and wife and child?
Loved ones who, in summers fled,
    Clung to him and wept and smiled?

"Reeling sinks the fated bark
    To her tomb beneath the wave:
Must he perish in the dark—
    Not a hand stretched out to save?

"See the spirits, how they crowd!
    Watching death with eyes that burn!
Waves rush in——" she shrieks aloud,
    Ere her waking sense return.

The storm is gone: the skies are clear:
    Hush'd is that bitter cry of pain:
The only sound, that meets her ear,
    The heaving of the sullen main.

Though heaviness endure the night,
    Yet joy shall come with break of day:

She shudders with a strange delight—
   The fearful dream is pass'd away.

She wakes: the grey dawn streaks the dark:
   With early song the copses ring:
Far off she hears the watch-dog bark
   A joyful bark of welcoming!

Feb. 23, 1857.

AFTER THREE DAYS

I stood within the gate
Of a great temple, 'mid the living stream
Of worshipers that thronged its regal state
Fair-pictured in my dream.

Jewels and gold were there;
And floors of marble lent a crystal sheen
To body forth, as in a lower air,
The wonders of the scene.

Such wild and lavish grace
Had whispers in it of a coming doom;
As richest flowers lie strown about the face
Of her that waits the tomb.

The wisest of the land
Had gathered there, three solemn trysting-days,
For high debate: men stood on either hand
To listen and to gaze.

The aged brows were bent,
Bent to a frown, half thought, and half annoy,
That all their stores of subtlest argument
Were baffled by a boy.

In each averted face
I marked but scorn and loathing, till mine eyes
Fell upon one that stirred not in his place,
Tranced in a dumb surprise.

Surely within his mind
Strange thoughts are born, until he doubts the lore
Of those old men, blind leaders of the blind,
Whose kingdom is no more.

Surely he sees afar
A day of death the stormy future brings;
The crimson setting of the herald-star
    That led the Eastern kings.

Thus, as a sunless deep
Mirrors the shining heights that crown the bay,
So did my soul create anew in sleep
    The picture seen by day.

Gazers came and went—
A restless hum of voices marked the spot—
In varying shades of critic discontent
    Prating they knew not what.

"Where is the comely limb,
The form attuned in every perfect part,
The beauty that we should desire in him?"
    Ah! Fools and slow of heart!

Look into those deep eyes,
Deep as the grave, and strong with love divine;
Those tender, pure, and fathomless mysteries,
    That seem to pierce through thine.

Look into those deep eyes,
Stirred to unrest by breath of coming strife,
Until a longing in thy soul arise
    That this indeed were life:

That thou couldst find Him there,
Bend at His sacred feet thy willing knee,
And from thy heart pour out the passionate prayer
    "Lord, let me follow Thee!"

But see the crowd divide:
Mother and sire have found their lost one now:
The gentle voice, that fain would seem to chide
    Whispers "Son, why hast thou"—

In tone of sad amaze—
"Thus dealt with us, that art our dearest thing?
Behold, thy sire and I, three weary days,
  Have sought thee sorrowing."

And I had stayed to hear
The loving words "How is it that ye sought?"—
But that the sudden lark, with matins clear,
  Severed the links of thought.

Then over all there fell
Shadow and silence; and my dream was fled,
As fade the phantoms of a wizard's cell
  When the dark charm is said.

Yet, in the gathering light,
I lay with half-shut eyes that would not wake,
Lovingly clinging to the skirts of night
  For that sweet vision's sake.

Feb. 16, 1861.

FACES IN THE FIRE

The night creeps onward, sad and slow:
In these red embers' dying glow
The forms of Fancy come and go.

An island-farm—broad seas of corn
Stirred by the wandering breath of morn—
The happy spot where I was born.

The picture fadeth in its place:
Amid the glow I seem to trace
The shifting semblance of a face.

'Tis now a little childish form—
Red lips for kisses pouted warm—
And elf-locks tangled in the storm.

'Tis now a grave and gentle maid,
At her own beauty half afraid,
Shrinking, and willing to be stayed.

Oh, Time was young, and Life was warm,
When first I saw that fairy-form,
Her dark hair tossing in the storm.

And fast and free these pulses played,
When last I met that gentle maid—
When last her hand in mine was laid.

Those locks of jet are turned to gray,
And she is strange and far away
That might have been mine own to-day—

That might have been mine own, my dear,
Through many and many a happy year—
That might have sat beside me here.

Ay, changeless through the changing scene,
The ghostly whisper rings between,
The dark refrain of 'might have been.'

The race is o'er I might have run:
The deeds are past I might have done;
And sere the wreath I might have won.

Sunk is the last faint flickering blaze:
The vision of departed days
Is vanished even as I gaze.

The pictures, with their ruddy light,
Are changed to dust and ashes white,
And I am left alone with night.

Jan., 1860.

A LESSON IN LATIN

Our Latin books, in motley row,
     Invite us to our task—
Gay Horace, stately Cicero:
Yet there's one verb, when once we know,
     No higher skill we ask:
This ranks all other lore above—
We've learned "'*Amare*' means '*to love*'!"

So, hour by hour, from flower to flower,
     We sip the sweets of Life:
Till, all too soon, the clouds arise,
And flaming cheeks and flashing eyes
     Proclaim the dawn of strife:
With half a smile and half a sigh,
"*Amare! Bitter One!*" we cry.

Last night we owned, with looks forlorn,
     "Too well the scholar knows
There is no rose without a thorn"—
But peace is made! We sing, this morn,
     "No thorn without a rose!"
Our Latin lesson is complete:
We've learned that Love is Bitter-Sweet!

May, 1888.

PUCK LOST AND FOUND

Puck has fled the haunts of men:
   Ridicule has made him wary:
In the woods, and down the glen,
      No one meets a Fairy!

"Cream!" the greedy Goblin cries—
   Empties the deserted dairy—
Steals the spoons, and off he flies.
      Still we seek our Fairy!

Ah! What form is entering?
   Lovelit eyes and laughter airy!
Is not this a better thing,
Child, whose visit thus I sing,
      Even than a Fairy?

Nov. 22, 1891.

Puck has ventured back agen:
   Ridicule no more affrights him:
In the very haunts of men
      Newer sport delights him.

Capering lightly to and fro,
   Ever frolicking and funning—
"Crack!" the mimic pistols go!
      Hark! The noise is stunning!

All too soon will Childhood gay
   Realise Life's sober sadness.
Let's be merry while we may,
Innocent and happy Fay!
      Elves were made for gladness!

Nov. 25, 1891.

A SONG OF LOVE

Say, what is the spell, when her fledgelings are cheeping,
　　That lures the bird home to her nest?
Or wakes the tired mother, whose infant is weeping,
　　To cuddle and croon it to rest?
What the magic that charms the glad babe in her arms,
　　Till it cooes with the voice of the dove?
'Tis a secret, and so let us whisper it low—
　　And the name of the secret is Love!
　　　　For I think it is Love,
　　　　For I feel it is Love,
　　For I'm sure it is nothing but Love!

Say, whence is the voice that, when anger is burning,
　　Bids the whirl of the tempest to cease?
That stirs the vexed soul with an aching—a yearning
　　For the brotherly hand-grip of peace?
Whence the music that fills all our being—that thrills
　　Around us, beneath, and above?
'Tis a secret: none knows how it comes, how it goes—
　　But the name of the secret is Love!
　　　　For I think it is Love,
　　　　For I feel it is Love,
　　For I'm sure it is nothing but Love!

Say, whose is the skill that paints valley and hill,
　　Like a picture so fair to the sight?
That flecks the green meadow with sunshine and shadow,
　　Till the little lambs leap with delight?
'Tis a secret untold to hearts cruel and cold,
　　Though 'tis sung, by the angels above,
In notes that ring clear for the ears that can hear—
　　And the name of the secret is Love!
　　　　For I think it is Love,
　　　　For I feel it is Love,
　　For I'm sure it is nothing but Love!

Oct., 1886.

Made in the USA
Monee, IL
07 July 2026

56555696R00031